LAUGH-OUT-LOUD JOKES

LAUGH-OUT-LOUD FAIRY TALE JOKES

BY LEONA FOWLER

WINDMILL BOOKS

Published in 2026 by Windmill Books, an Imprint of Rosen Publishing
2544 Clinton St., Buffalo, NY 14224

First Edition

Editor: Caitie McAneney
Book Design: Claire Zimmermann

Photo Credits: Cover, p.1 (child reading) Master1305/Shutterstock.com; series art (paper texture) OanaGherghe2/Shutterstock.com; series art (illustrations throughout) Look_Studio/Shutterstock.com; cover, pp. 1, 20 (fairy illustration) Nadzin/Shutterstock.com; p. 5, 7, 11, 13, 15, 17, 19, 21 AI Generated/Shutterstock.com; p. 9 Pushkin/Shutterstock.com.

Some of the images in this book illustrate individuals who are models. The depictions do not imply actual situations or events.

Library of Congress Cataloging-in-Publication Data

Names: Fowler, Leona.
Title: Fairy tale jokes / Leona Fowler.
Description: Buffalo, NY : Windmill Books, 2026. | Series: Laugh-out-loud jokes | Includes glossary and index.
Identifiers: ISBN 9781538399194 (pbk.) | ISBN 9781538399200 (library bound) | ISBN 9781538399217 (ebook)
Subjects: LCSH: Fairy tales–Juvenile humor. | Wit and humor, Juvenile.
Classification: LCC PN6231.F285 F69 2026 | DDC 818.'602–dc23

Manufactured in the United States of America

CPSIA Compliance Information: Batch #CSWM26. For further information, contact Rosen Publishing at 1-800-237-9932

CONTENTS

Words in the glossary appear in **bold** the first time they are used in the text.

CHARACTERS WITH A TWIST

What do you call a wooden puppet who lives on a farm?

PIGNOCCHIO.

What do you get when you cross a fairy tale villain and a lumberjack?

THE BIG PLAID WOLF.

What did the princess call the evil mosquito?

THE WICKED ITCH.

Who grants the wishes of animals?

THE FAIRY DOGMOTHER.

FUN FACT!

Fairy tales and **fables** often **feature** a "Big Bad Wolf," such as "Little Red Riding Hood" and "The Three Little Pigs." However, in real life, wolves usually keep to themselves.

SILLY CINDERELLA

Why did Cinderella lose the basketball game?

SHE RAN AWAY FROM THE BALL.

Why did the prince give Cinderella her glass slipper?

SHE WAS HIS SOLE MATE.

Why was Cinderella bad at tennis?

HER COACH WAS A PUMPKIN.

What do you get when you mix cheese and a fairy tale princess?

MOZZA-RELLA!

FUN FACT!

Stories featuring Cinderella are hundreds of years old, told in many countries. However, the Disney film "Cinderella" came out in 1950.

RAPUNZEL RIDDLES

How did Rapunzel feel after her haircut?

A BIT LIGHT-HEADED.

Is Rapunzel a fairy tale?

NO, IT'S A HAIRY TALE!

What did the prince say to get Rapunzel to come to a party?

"LET YOUR HAIR DOWN AND LIVE A LITTLE!"

Who won the princess race?

RAPUNZEL WON, BY A HAIR.

FUN FACT!

The story of Rapunzel became popular after it was included in the *Children's and Household Tales* collection by the Brothers Grimm in 1812.

CLASSIC TALES

Why did Hansel and Gretel get lost in the woods?

THE TRAIL WAS CRUMBY.

When did the Ugly Duckling turn into a swan?

AT THE QUACK OF DAWN.

Why was the giant at the top of the beanstalk bad at football?

HE ALWAYS FEE-FI-FO-FUMBLED!

Why couldn't Goldilocks sleep?

SHE HAD NIGHT-BEARS!

FUN FACT!

"Jack and the Beanstalk" is an English fairy tale in which a boy climbs a magical beanstalk and meets a deadly giant.

PRINCESS PUNS

What happens when you give a princess a broom?

SHE TURNS INTO SWEEPING BEAUTY.

Why did the princess go to the dentist?

SHE BROKE HER CROWN!

Do princesses drink coffee?

NO, THEY PREFER ROYAL TEA.

Did you hear the story about the princess and the frog?

IT'S RIBBETING.

FUN FACT!

"The Frog Prince" is a fairy tale by the Brothers Grimm, in which a princess meets a frog, who is actually a prince.

UNDER THE SEA

What did the ocean say to the Little Mermaid?

NOTHING, IT JUST WAVED.

What did the Little Mermaid ride to the ball?

A SEAHORSE.

Why did the Little Mermaid want to stop being human?

SHE GOT COLD FEET.

Where do mermaids sleep?

IN WATERBEDS.

FUN FACT!

"The Little Mermaid" was a fairy tale written by Danish author Hans Christian Anderson in 1837.

WHICH WITCH?

Which fairy tale character would you find on a beach?

A SAND WITCH.

Did the witch ever leave the kingdom?

YES, SHE ONLY STAYED FOR A SPELL.

How do you make a witch itch?

TAKE AWAY THE W!

What's the problem with twin witches?

YOU CAN NEVER TELL WHICH WITCH IS WHICH.

FUN FACT!

Many fairy tales and **folktales** around the world include a witch character. Some stories show them as evil, helpful, respected, powerful, or some mix of those traits.

EGGCELLENT JOKES

How did Humpty Dumpty get down the wall so quickly?

HE SCRAMBLED.

Did you hear the one about Humpty Dumpty?

NO, IT'S AN INSIDE YOLK.

Why did the magical golden egg hide?

IT WAS A LITTLE CHICKEN!

What did Snow White name her hen?

EGG WHITE.

FUN FACT!

Humpty Dumpty was pictured as an egg in 1871 in Lewis Carol's book Through the Looking Glass and What Alice Found There.

FUNNY FAIRIES

What do you call a fairy with great ideas?

THINKER BELL.

Which fairy lives in the ocean?

THE FAIRY CODMOTHER.

Why was the fairy picture such low quality?

IT WAS ALL PIXIE-LATED!

What kind of picture did the fairy take?

AN ELFIE!

FUN FACT!

In different cultures and stories, fairies have been called different things, including sprites, faeries, pixies, and elves. Some are seen as good, while others make trouble.

GLOSSARY

crown: A band or covering for the head; also, a part of a tooth.

fable: A short story, especially one that means to teach a lesson and in which animals act like humans.

feature: To play an important part.

folktale: A story made up and handed down by the common people.

fumble: In football, to drop the football while it is still in play.

plaid: A pattern printed on cloth with Scottish origins, often worn for outdoorsy activities and jobs.

sole: The bottom of a foot or shoe.

villain: A person who does bad things.

FOR MORE INFORMATION

BOOKS

Rewse, Katie. *Cinderella.* Buffalo NY: Windmill Books, 2024.

Tika and Tata. *Sleeping Beauty.* Buffalo, NY: Windmill Books, 2024.

WEBSITES

Fairy Tale
kids.britannica.com/students/article/fairy-tale/274256
Learn more about fairy tales and their magical themes with Britannica Kids.

Grimm Brothers
kids.britannica.com/kids/article/Grimm-Brothers/353216
Meet the Brothers Grimm, the writers behind the classic fairy tale characters Cinderella, Rapunzel, and more.

INDEX